MICHAEL LONGLEY

Selected Poems

BY THE SAME AUTHOR

POETRY

No Continuing City
An Exploded View
Man Lying on a Wall
The Echo Gate
Selected Poems 1963–1980
Poems 1963–1983
Gorse Fires
The Ghost Orchid

AUTOBIOGRAPHY

Tuppenny Stung

AS EDITOR

Causeway: The Arts in Ulster
Under the Moon, Over the Stars: Children's Poetry
Further Reminiscences: Paul Henry
Selected Poems: Louis MacNeice
Poems: W. R. Rodgers

MICHAEL LONGLEY

Selected Poems

Wake Forest University Press

First U.S. Edition published 1999
Published in association with Cape Poetry,
Random House UK, London.

Wake Forest University Press
Post Office Box 7333, Winston-Salem,
NC 27109

Typeset by Palimpsest Book Production Ltd
Printed in the
United States by Thomson-Shore, Inc.

Library of Congress card 98-61875
ISBN (cloth) 0-916390-90-x
ISBN (paperback) 0-916390-89-6

Wake Forest University Press

CONTENTS

For Eamonn Hughes & Bob Purdie

When all the reeds are swaying in the wind
How can you tell which reeds the otters bend?

EPITHALAMION

These are the small hours when
Moths by their fatal appetite
That brings them tapping to get in,
Are steered along the night
To where our window catches light.

Who hazard all to be
Where we, the only two it seems,
Inhabit so delightfully
A room it bursts its seams
And spills on to the lawn in beams,

Such visitors as these
Reflect with eyes like frantic stars
This garden's brightest properties,
Cruising its corridors
Of light above the folded flowers,

Till our vicinity
Is rendered royal by their flight
Towards us, till more silently
The silent stars ignite,
Their aeons dwindling by a night,

And everything seems bent
On robing in this evening you
And me, all dark the element
Our light is earnest to,
All quiet gathered round us who,

When over the embankments
A train that's loudly reprobate
Shoots from silence into silence,
With ease accommodate
Its pandemonium, its freight.

I hold you close because
We have decided dark will be
For ever like this and because,
My love, already
The dark is growing elderly.

With dawn upon its way,
Punctually and as a rule,
The small hours widening into day,
Our room its vestibule
Before it fills all houses full,

We too must hazard all,
Switch off the lamp without a word
For the last of night assembled
Over it and unperturbed
By the moth that lies there littered,

And notice how the trees
Which took on anonymity
Are again in their huge histories
Displayed, that wherever we
Attempt, and as far as we can see,

The flowers everywhere
Are withering, the stars dissolved,
Amalgamated in a glare,
Which last night were revolved
Discreetly round us – and, involved,

The two of us, in these
Which early morning has deformed,
Must hope that in new properties
We'll find a uniform
To know each other truly by, or,

At the least, that these will,
When we rise, be seen with dawn
As remnant yet part raiment still,
Like flags that linger on
The sky when king and queen are gone.

NO CONTINUING CITY

My hands here, gentle, where her breasts begin,
My picture in her eyes –
It is time for me to recognise
This new dimension, my last girl.
So, to set my house in order, I imagine
Photographs, advertisements – the old lies,
The lumber of my soul –

All that is due for spring cleaning,
Everything that soul-destroys.
Into the open I bring
Girls who linger still in photostat
(For whom I was so many different boys) –
I explode their myths before it is too late,
Their promises I detonate –

There is quite a lot that I can do . . .
I leave them – are they six or seven, two or three? –
Locked in their small geographies.
The hillocks of their bodies' lovely shires
(Whose all weathers I have walked through)
Acre by acre recede entire
To summer country.

From collision to eclipse their case is closed.
Who took me by surprise
Like comets first – now, failing to ignite,
They constellate such uneventful skies,
Their stars arranged each night
In the old stories
Which I successfully have diagnosed.

Though they momentarily survive
In my delays,
They neither cancel nor improve
My continuing city with old ways,
Familiar avenues to love –
Down my one-way streets (it is time to finish)
Their eager syllables diminish.

Though they call out from the suburbs
Of experience – they know how that disturbs! –
Or, already tending towards home,
Prepare to hitch-hike on the kerbs,
Their bags full of dear untruths –
I am their medium
And I take the words out of their mouths.

From today new hoardings crowd my eyes,
Pasted over my ancient histories
Which (I must be cruel to be kind)
Only gale or cloudburst now discover,
Ripping the billboard of my mind –
Oh, there my lovers,
There my dead no longer advertise.

I transmit from the heart a closing broadcast
To my girl, my bride, my wife-to-be –
I tell her she is welcome,
Advising her to make this last,
To be sure of finding room in me
(I embody bed and breakfast) –
To eat and drink me out of house and home.

CIRCE

The cries of the shipwrecked enter my head.
On wildest nights when the torn sky confides
Its face to the sea's cracked mirror, my bed
– Addressed by the moon and her tutored tides –

Through brainstorm, through nightmare and ocean
Keeps me afloat. Shallows are my coven,
The comfortable margins – in this notion
I stand uncorrected by the sun even.

Out of the night husband after husband
– Eyes wide as oysters, arms full of driftwood –
Wades ashore and puts in at my island.
My necklaces of sea shells and seaweed,

My skirts of spindrift, sandals of flotsam
Catch the eye of each bridegroom for ever.
Quite forgetful of the widowing calm
My sailors wait through bad and good weather.

At first in rock pools I become their wife,
Under the dunes at last they lie with me –
These are the spring and neap tides of their life.
I have helped so many sailors off the sea,

And, counting no man among my losses,
I have made of my arms and my thighs last rooms
For the irretrievable and capsized –
I extend the sea, its idioms.

PERSEPHONE

I

I see as through a skylight in my brain
The mole strew its buildings in the rain,

The swallows turn above their broken home
And all my acres in delirium.

II

Straitjacketed by cold and numskulled
Now sleep the welladjusted and the skilled –

The bat folds its wing like a winter leaf,
The squirrel in its hollow holds aloof.

III

The weasel and ferret, the stoat and fox
Move hand in glove across the equinox.

I can tell how softly their footsteps go –
Their footsteps borrow silence from the snow.

NAUSICAA

You scarcely raise a finger to the tide.
Pavilions, those days off at the seaside

Collapse about your infinite arrest –
He sees your cove more clearly than the rest.

All evidence of dry land he relearns.
The ocean gathers where your shoulder turns.

NARCISSUS

Unweatherbeaten as the moon my face
Among the waterlogged, the commonplace,

Old boots and kettles for inheritance
Drifting into my head on the off-chance –

A wide Sargasso where the names of things
(Important guests at all such christenings)

Submerge in mind and pool like treasure-trove.
My face as sole survivor floats above.

A PERSONAL STATEMENT

for Seamus Heaney

Since you, Mind, think to diagnose
Experience
As summer, satin, nightingale or rose,
Of the senses making sense –
Follow my nose,

Attend all other points of contact,
Deserve your berth:
My brain-child, help me find my own way back
To fire, air, water, earth.
I am, in fact,

More than a bag of skin and bone.
My person is
A chamber where the elements postpone
In lively synthesis,
In peace on loan,

Old wars of flood and earthquake, storm
And holocaust,
Their attributes most temperately reformed
Of heatwave and of frost.
They take my form,

Learn from my arteries their pace –
They leave alarms
And excursions for my heart and lungs to face.
I hold them in my arms
And keep in place.

To walk, to run, to leap, to stand –
Of the litany
Of movement I the vicar in command,
The prophet in my country,
The priest at hand,

Take steps to make it understood
The occupants
Assembled here in narrow neighbourhood
Are my constituents
For bad or good.

Body and Mind, I turn to you.
It's me you fit.
Whatever you think, whatever you do,
Include me in on it,
Essential Two.

Who house philosophy and force,
Wed well in me
The elements, for fever's their divorce,
Nightmare and ecstasy,
And death of course.

My sponsor, Mind, my satellite,
Keep my balance,
Steer me through my heyday, through my night,
My senses' common sense,
Selfcentred light.

And you who set me in my ways,
Immaculate,
In full possession of my faculties –
Till you disintegrate,
Exist to please.

Lest I with fears and hopes capsize,
By your own lights
Sail, Body, cargoless towards surprise.
And come, Mind, raise your sights –
Believe my eyes.

FREEZE-UP

The freeze-up annexes the sea even,
Putting out over the waves its platform.
Let skies fall, the fox's belly cave in –
This catastrophic shortlived reform
Directs to our homes the birds of heaven.
They come on farfetched winds to keep us warm.

Bribing these with bounty, we would rather
Forget our hopes of thaw when spring will clean
The boughs, dust from our sills snow and feather,
Release to its decay and true decline
The bittern whom this different weather
Cupboarded in ice like a specimen.

THE OSPREY

To whom certain water talents –
Webbed feet, oils – do not occur,
Regulates his liquid acre
From the sky, his proper element.

There, already, his eye removes
The trout each fathom magnifies.
He lives, without compromise,
His unamphibious two lives –

An inextinguishable bird whom
No lake's waters waterlog.
He shakes his feathers like a dog.
It's all of air that ferries him.

THE HEBRIDES

for Eavan Boland

I

The winds' enclosure, Atlantic's premises,
        Last balconies
    Above the waves, The Hebrides –
        Too long did I postpone
Presbyterian granite and the lack of trees,
        This orphaned stone

Day in, day out colliding with the sea.
        Weather forecast,
    Compass nor ordnance survey
        Arranges my welcome
For, on my own, I have lost my way at last,
        So far from home.

In whom the city is continuing,
        I stop to look,
    To find my feet among the ling
        And bracken – over me
The bright continuum of gulls, a rook
        Occasionally.

II

My eyes, slowly accepting panorama,
        Try to include
    In my original idea
        The total effect
Of air and ocean – waterlogged all wood –
        All harbours wrecked –

My dead-lights latched by whelk and barnacle
Till I abide
By the sea wall of the time I kill –
My each nostalgic scheme
Jettisoned, as crises are, the further side
Of sleep and dream.

Between wind and wave this holiday
The cormorant,
The oyster-catcher and osprey
Proceed and keep in line
While I, hands in my pockets, hesitant,
Am in two minds.

III

Old neighbours, though shipwreck's my decision,
People my brain –
Like breakwaters against the sun,
Command in silhouette
My island circumstance – my cells retain,
Perpetuate

Their crumpled deportment through bad weather.
And I feel them
Put on their raincoats for ever
And walk out in the sea.
I am, though each one waves a phantom limb,
The amputee,

For these are my sailors, these my drowned –
In their heart of hearts,
In their city I ran aground.
Along my arteries
Sluice those homewaters petroleum hurts.
Dry dock, gantries,

Dykes of apparatus educate my bones
        To track the buoys
  Up sea lanes love emblazons
      To streets where shall conclude
My journey back from flux to poise, from poise
        To attitude.

Here, at the edge of my experience,
        Another tide
  Along the broken shore extends
      A lifetime's wrack and ruin –
No flotsam I may beachcomb now can hide
        That water line.

IV

Beyond the lobster pots where plankton spreads
        Porpoises turn.
  Seals slip over the cockle beds.
      Undertow dishevels
Seaweed in the shallows – and I discern
        My sea levels.

To right and left of me there intervene
        The tumbled burns –
  And these, on turf and boulder weaned,
      Confuse my calendar –
Their tilt is suicidal, their great return
        Curricular.

No matter what repose holds shore and sky
        In harmony,
  From this place in the long run I,
      Though here I might have been
Content with rivers where they meet the sea,
        Remove upstream,

Where the salmon, risking fastest waters –
Waterfall and rock
And the effervescent otters –
On bridal pools insist
As with fin and generation they unlock
The mountain's fist.

V

Now, buttoned up, with water in my shoes,
Clouds around me,
I can, through mist that misconstrues,
Read like a palimpsest
My past – those landmarks and that scenery
I dare resist.

Into my mind's unsympathetic trough
They fade away –
And to alter my perspective
I feel in the sharp cold
Of my vantage point too high above the bay
The sea grow old.

Granting the trawlers far below their stance,
Their anchorage,
I fight all the way for balance –
In the mountain's shadow
Losing foothold, covet the privilege
Of vertigo.

IN MEMORIAM

My father, let no similes eclipse
Where crosses like some forest simplified
Sink roots into my mind; the slow sands
Of your history delay till through your eyes
I read you like a book. Before you died,
Re-enlisting with all the broken soldiers
You bent beneath your rucksack, near collapse,
In anecdote rehearsed and summarised
These words I write in memory. Let yours
And other heartbreaks play into my hands.

Now I see in close-up, in my mind's eye,
The cracked and splintered dead for pity's sake
Each dismal evening predecease the sun,
You, looking death and nightmare in the face
With your kilt, harmonica and gun,
Grow older in a flash, but none the wiser
(Who, following the wrong queue at The Palace,
Have joined the London Scottish by mistake),
Your nineteen years uncertain if and why
Belgium put the kibosh on the Kaiser.

Between the corpses and the soup canteens
You swooned away, watching your future spill.
But, as it was, your proper funeral urn
Had mercifully smashed to smithereens,
To sharpnel shards that sliced your testicle.
That instant I, your most unlikely son,
In No Man's Land was surely left for dead,
Blotted out from your far horizon.
As your voice now is locked inside my head,
I yet was held secure, waiting my turn.

Finally, that lousy war was over.
Stranded in France and in need of proof
You hunted down experimental lovers,
Persuading chorus girls and countesses:
This, father, the last confidence you spoke.
In my twentieth year your old wounds woke
As cancer. Lodging under the same roof
Death was a visitor who hung about,
Strewing the house with pills and bandages,
Till he chose to put your spirit out.

Though they overslept the sequence of events
Which ended with the ambulance outside,
You lingering in the hall, your bowels on fire,
Tears in your eyes, and all your medals spent,
I summon girls who packed at last and went
Underground with you. Their souls again on hire,
Now those lost wives as recreated brides
Take shape before me, materialise.
On the verge of light and happy legend
They lift their skirts like blinds across your eyes.

ELEGY FOR FATS WALLER

for Solly Lipsitz

Lighting up, lest all our hearts should break,
His fiftieth cigarette of the day,
Happy with so many notes at his beck
And call, he sits there taking it away,
The maker of immaculate slapstick.

With music and with such precise rampage
Across the deserts of the blues a trail
He blazes, towards the one true mirage,
Enormous on a nimble-footed camel
And almost refusing to be his age.

He plays for hours on end and though there be
Oases one part water, two parts gin,
He tumbles past to reign, wise and thirsty,
At the still centre of his loud dominion –
THE SHOOK THE SHAKE THE SHEIKH OF ARABY.

HOMAGE TO DR JOHNSON
for Philip Hobsbaum

I

The Hebridean gales mere sycophants,
So many loyal Boswells at his heel –
Yet the farflung outposts of experience
In the end undo a Roman wall,

The measured style. London is so far;
Each windswept strait he would encompass
Gives the unsinkable lexicographer
His reflection in its shattered glass.

He trudges off in the mist and the rain
Where only the thickest skin survives,
Among the rocks construes himself again,
Lifts through those altering perspectives

His downcast eyes, riding out the brainstorm,
His weatherproof enormous head at home.

II

There was no place to go but his own head
Where hard luck lodged as in an orphanage
With the desperate and the underfed.

So, surgeon himself to his dimensions,
The words still unembarrassed by their size,
He corrected death in its declensions,

The waters breaking where he stabbed the knife,
Washing his pockmarked body like a reef.

LEAVING INISHMORE

Rain and sunlight and the boat between them
Shifted whole hillsides through the afternoon –
Quiet variations on an urgent theme
Reminding me now that we left too soon
The island awash in wave and anthem.

Miles from the brimming enclave of the bay
I hear again the Atlantic's voices,
The gulls above us as we pulled away –
So munificent their final noises
These are the broadcasts from our holiday.

Oh, the crooked walkers on that tilting floor!
And the girls singing on the upper deck
Whose hair took the light like a downpour –
Interim nor change of scene shall shipwreck
Those folk on the move between shore and shore.

Summer and solstice as the seasons turn
Anchor our boat in a perfect standstill,
The harbour wall of Inishmore astern
Where the Atlantic waters overspill –
I shall name this the point of no return

Lest that excursion out of light and heat
Take on a January idiom –
Our ocean icebound when the year is hurt,
Wintertime past cure – the curriculum
Vitae of sailors and the sick at heart.

JOURNEY OUT OF ESSEX
or, John Clare's Escape from the Madhouse

I am lying with my head
Over the edge of the world,
Unpicking my whereabouts
Like the asylum's name
That they stitch on the sheets.

Sick now with bad weather
Or a virus from the fens,
I dissolve in a puddle
My biographies of birds
And the names of flowers.

That they may recuperate
Alongside the stunned mouse,
The hedgehog rolled in leaves,
I am putting to bed
In this rheumatic ditch

The boughs of my harvest-home,
My wives, one on either side,
And keeping my head low as
A lark's nest, my feet toward
Helpston and the pole star.

CARAVAN

A rickety chimney suggests
The diminutive stove,
Children perhaps, the pots
And pans adding up to love –

So much concentrated under
The low roof, the windows
Shuttered against snow and wind,
That you would be magnified

(If you were there) by the dark,
Wearing it like an apron
And revolving in your hands
As weather in a glass dome,

The blizzard, the day beyond
And – tiny, barely in focus –
Me disappearing out of view
On probably the only horse,

Cantering off to the right
To collect the week's groceries,
Or to be gone for good
Having drawn across my eyes

Like a curtain all that light
And the snow, my history
Stiffening with the tea towels
Hung outside the door to dry.

SWANS MATING

Even now I wish that you had been there
Sitting beside me on the riverbank:
The cob and his pen sailing in rhythm
Until their small heads met and the final
Heraldic moment dissolved in ripples.

This was a marriage and a baptism,
A holding of breath, nearly a drowning,
Wings spread wide for balance where he trod,
Her feathers full of water and her neck
Under the water like a bar of light.

GALAPAGOS

Now you have scattered into islands –
Breasts, belly, knees, the mount of Venus,
Each a Galapagos of the mind
Where you, the perfect stranger, prompter
Of throw-backs, of hold-ups in time,

Embody peculiar animals –
The giant tortoise hesitating,
The shy lemur, the iguana's
Slow gaze in which the *Beagle* anchors
With its homesick scientist on board.

THE CORNER OF THE EYE

kingfisher

a knife-thrower
hurling himself, a rainbow
fractured against
the plate glass of winter:

his eye a water bead,
lens and meniscus where
the dragonfly drowns,
the water-boatman crawls.

wren

two wings criss-crossing
through gaps and loop-holes,
a mote melting towards
the corner of the eye:

or poised in the thicket
between adulteries,
small spaces circumscribed
by the tilt of his tail.

dipper

the cataract's deluge
and nightmare a curtain
he can go behind,
heavy water rolling

over feather and eye
its adhesive drops,
beneath his feet the spray
thickening into moss.

robin

breast a warning, he
shadows the heavy-
footed earth-breakers,
bull's hoof, pheasant's toe:

is an eye that would –
if we let it in – scan
the walls for cockroaches,
for bed-bugs the beds.

BADGER

for Raymond Piper

I

Pushing the wedge of his body
Between cromlech and stone circle,
He excavates down mine shafts
And back into the depths of the hill.

His path straight and narrow
And not like the fox's zig-zags,
The arc of the hare who leaves
A silhouette on the sky line.

Night's silence around his shoulders,
His face lit by the moon, he
Manages the earth with his paws,
Returns underground to die.

II

An intestine taking in
patches of dog's-mercury,
brambles, the bluebell wood;
a heel revolving acorns;
a head with a price on it
brushing cuckoo-spit, goose-grass;
a name that parishes borrow.

III

For the digger, the earth-dog
It is a difficult delivery
Once the tongs take hold,

Vulnerable his pig's snout
That lifted cow-pats for beetles,
Hedgehogs for the soft meat,

His limbs dragging after them
So many stones turned over,
The trees they tilted.

CASUALTY

Its decline was gradual,
A sequence of explorations
By other animals, each
Looking for the easiest way in –

A surgical removal of the eyes,
A probing of the orifices,
Bitings down through the skin,
Through tracts where the grasses melt,

And the bad air released
In a ceremonious wounding
So slow that more and more
I wanted to get closer to it.

A candid grin, the bones
Accumulating to a diagram
Except for the polished horns,
The immaculate hooves.

And this no final reduction
For the ribs began to scatter,
The wool to move outward
As though hunger still worked there,

As though something that had followed
Fox and crow was desperate for
A last morsel and was
Other than the wind or rain.

READINGS

for Peter Longley

I

I remember your eyes in bandages
And me reading to you like a mother;
Our grubby redeemer, the chimney-sweep
Whose baptism among the seaweed
Began when he stopped astounded beside
The expensive bed, the white coverlet,
The most beautiful girl he had ever seen –
Her hair on the eiderdown like algae,
Her face a reflection in clean water;
The Irishwoman haunting Tom's shoulder –
The shawl's canopy, the red petticoats
Arriving beside him again and again,
The white feet accompanying his feet,
All of the leafy roads down to the sea.

II

Other faces at the frosty window,
Kay and Gerda in their separate attics;
The icicle driven into Kay's heart –
Then a glance at the pillow where you
Twisted your head again and tried to squeeze
Light like a tear through the bandages.

LETTER TO DEREK MAHON

And did we come into our own
When, minus muse and lexicon,
We traced in August sixty-nine
Our imaginary Peace Line
Around the burnt-out houses of
The Catholics we'd scarcely loved,
Two Sisyphuses come to budge
The sticks and stones of an old grudge,

Two poetic conservatives
In the city of guns and long knives,
Our ears receiving then and there
The stereophonic nightmare
Of the Shankill and the Falls,
Our matches struck on crumbling walls
To light us as we moved at last
Through the back alleys of Belfast?

Why it mattered to have you here
You who journeyed to Inisheer
With me, years back, one Easter when
With MacIntyre and the lone Dane
Our footsteps lifted up the larks,
Echoing off those western rocks
And down that darkening arcade
Hung with the failures of our trade,

Will understand. We were tongue-tied
Companions of the island's dead
In the graveyard among the dunes,
Eavesdroppers on conversations
With a Jesus who spoke Irish –
We were strangers in that parish,
Black tea with bacon and cabbage
For our sacraments and pottage,

Dank blankets making up our Lent
Till, islanders ourselves, we bent
Our knees and cut the watery sod
From the lazy-bed where slept a God
We couldn't count among our friends,
Although we'd taken in our hands
Splinters of driftwood nailed and stuck
On the rim of the Atlantic.

That was Good Friday years ago –
How persistent the undertow
Slapped by currachs ferrying stones,
Moonlight glossing the confusions
Of its each bilingual wave – yes,
We would have lingered there for less . . .
Six islanders for a ten-bob note
Rowed us out to the anchored boat.

LETTER TO SEAMUS HEANEY

From Carrigskeewaun in Killadoon
I write, although I'll see you soon,
Hoping this fortnight detonates
Your year in the United States,
Offering you by way of welcome
To the sick counties we call home
The mystical point at which I tire
Of Calor gas and a turf fire.

Till we talk again in Belfast
Pleasanter far to leave the past
Across three acres and two brooks
On holiday in a post box
Which dripping fuchsia bells surround,
Its back to the prevailing wind,
And where sanderlings from Iceland
Court the breakers, take my stand,

Disinfecting with a purer air
That small subconscious cottage where
The Irish poet slams his door
On slow-worm, toad and adder:
Beneath these racing skies it is
A tempting stance indeed – *ipsis*
Hibernicis hiberniores –
Except that we know the old stories,

The midden of cracked hurley sticks
Tied to recall the crucifix,
Of broken bones and lost scruples,
The blackened hearth, the blazing gable's
Telltale cinder where we may
Scorch our shins until that day
We sleepwalk through a No Man's Land
Lipreading to an Orange band.

Continually, therefore, we rehearse
Goodbyes to all our characters
And, since both would have it both ways,
On the oily roll of calmer seas
Launch coffin-ship and life-boat,
Body with soul thus kept afloat,
Mind open like a half-door
To the speckled hill, the plovers' shore.

So let it be the lapwing's cry
That lodges in the throat as I
Raise its alarum from the mud,
Seeking for your sake to conclude
Ulster Poet our Union Title
And prolong this sad recital
By leaving careful footprints round
A wind-encircled burial mound.

WOUNDS

Here are two pictures from my father's head –
I have kept them like secrets until now:
First, the Ulster Division at the Somme
Going over the top with 'Fuck the Pope!'
'No Surrender!': a boy about to die,
Screaming 'Give 'em one for the Shankill!'
'Wilder than Gurkhas' were my father's words
Of admiration and bewilderment.
Next comes the London-Scottish padre
Resettling kilts with his swagger-stick,
With a stylish backhand and a prayer.
Over a landscape of dead buttocks
My father followed him for fifty years.
At last, a belated casualty,
He said – lead traces flaring till they hurt –
'I am dying for King and Country, slowly.'
I touched his hand, his thin head I touched.

Now, with military honours of a kind,
With his badges, his medals like rainbows,
His spinning compass, I bury beside him
Three teenage soldiers, bellies full of
Bullets and Irish beer, their flies undone.
A packet of Woodbines I throw in,
A lucifer, the Sacred Heart of Jesus
Paralysed as heavy guns put out
The night-light in a nursery for ever;
Also a bus-conductor's uniform –
He collapsed beside his carpet-slippers
Without a murmur, shot through the head
By a shivering boy who wandered in
Before they could turn the television down
Or tidy away the supper dishes.
To the children, to a bewildered wife,
I think 'Sorry Missus' was what he said.

IN MEMORY OF GERARD DILLON

I

You walked, all of a sudden, through
The rickety gate which opens
To a scatter of curlews,
An acre of watery light; your grave
A dip in the dunes where sand mislays
The sound of the sea, earth over you
Like a low Irish sky; the sun
An electric light bulb clouded
By the sandy tides, sunlight lost
And found, a message in a bottle.

II

You are a room full of self-portraits,
A face that follows us everywhere;
An ear to the ground listening for
Dead brothers in layers; an eye
Taking in the beautiful predators –
Cats on the windowsill, birds of prey
And, between the diminutive fields,
A dragonfly, wings full of light
Where the road narrows to the last farm.

III

Christening robes, communion dresses,
The shawls of factory workers,
A blind drawn on the Lower Falls.

THE WEST

Beneath a gas-mantle that the moths bombard,
Light that powders at a touch, dusty wings,
I listen for news through the atmospherics,
A crackle of sea-wrack, spinning driftwood,
Waves like distant traffic, news from home,

Or watch myself, as through a sandy lens,
Materialising out of the heat-shimmers
And finding my way for ever along
The path to this cottage, its windows,
Walls, sun and moon dials, home from home.

SKARA BRAE

for Sheila and Denis Smyth

A window into the ground,
The bumpy lawn in section,
An exploded view
Through middens, through lives,

The thatch of grass roots,
The gravelly roof compounding
Periwinkles, small bones,
A calendar of meals,

The thread between sepulchre
And home a broken necklace,
Knuckles, dice scattering
At the warren's core,

Pebbles the tide washes
That conceded for so long
Living room, the hard beds,
The table made of stone.

GHOST TOWN

I have located it, my ghost town –
A place of interminable afternoons,
Sad cottages, scythes rusting in the thatch;
Of so many hesitant surrenders to
Enfolding bog, the scuts of bog cotton.

The few residents include one hermit
Persisting with a goat and two kettles
Among the bracken, a nervous spinster
In charge of the post office, a lighthouse-keeper
Who emerges to collect his groceries.

Since no one has got around to it yet
I shall restore the sign which reads CINEMA,
Rescue from the verge of invisibility
The faded stills of the last silent feature –
I shall become the local eccentric:

Already I have retired there to fill
Several gaps in my education –
The weather's ways, a handful of neglected
Pentatonic melodies and, after a while,
Dialect words for the parts of the body.

Indeed, with so much on my hands, family
And friends are definitely not welcome –
Although by the time I am accepted there
(A reputation and my own half-acre)
I shall have written another letter home.

THREE POSTHUMOUS PIECES

I

In lieu of my famous last words or
The doctor's hushed diagnosis
Lifting like a draught from the door
My oracular pages, this
Will have fluttered on to the floor –
The first of my posthumous pieces.

II

As a sort of accompaniment
Drafted in different-coloured inks
Through several notebooks, this is meant
To read like a riddle from the Sphinx
And not my will and testament –
No matter what anybody thinks.

III

Two minuses become a plus
When, at the very close of play
And with the minimum of fuss,
I shall permit myself to say:
This is my Opus Posthumous –
An inspiration in its way.

ALIBIS

I

My botanical studies took me among
Those whom I now consider my ancestors.
I used to appear to them at odd moments –
With buckets of water in the distance, or
At the campfire, my arms full of snowy sticks.
Beech mast, hedgehogs, cresses were my diet,
My medicaments badger grease and dock leaves.
A hard life. Nevertheless, they named after me
A clover that flourished on those distant slopes.
Later I found myself playing saxophone
On the Souza Band's Grand Tour of the World.
Perhaps because so much was happening
I started, in desperation, to keep a diary.
(I have no idea what came over me.)
After that I sat near a sunny window
Waiting for pupils among the music-stands.
At present I am drafting appendices
To lost masterpieces, some of them my own –
Requiems, entertainments for popes and kings.
From time to time I choose to express myself
In this manner, the basic line. Indeed,
My one remaining ambition is to be
The last poet in Europe to find a rhyme.

II

I wanted this to be a lengthy meditation
With myself as the central character –
Official guide through the tall pavilions
Or even the saviour of damaged birds.
I accepted my responsibilities
And was managing daily after matins
And before lunch my stint of composition.

But gradually, as though I had planned it,
And with only a few more pages to go
Of my *Apologia Pro Vita Mea*,
There dawned on me this idea of myself
Clambering aboard an express train full of
Honeymoon couples and football supporters.
I had folded my life like a cheque book,
Wrapped my pyjamas around two noggins
To keep, for a while at least, my visions warm.
Tattered and footloose in my final phase
I improvised on the map of the world
And hurtled to join, among the police files,
My obstreperous bigfisted brothers.

III

I could always have kept myself to myself
And, falling asleep with the light still on,
Reached the quiet conclusion that this
(And this is where I came in) was no more than
The accommodation of different weathers,
Whirlwind tours around the scattered islands,
Telephone calls from the guilty suburbs,
From the back of the mind, a simple question
Of being in two places at the one time.

OPTIONS

for Michael Allen

> *Ha! here's three on's are sophisticated.*
> *Thou art the thing itself.*

These were my options: firstly
To have gone on and on –
A garrulous correspondence
Between me, the ideal reader
And – a halo to high-light
My head – that outer circle
Of critical intelligences
Deciphering – though with telling
Lacunae – my life-story,
Holding up to the bright mirrors
Of expensive libraries
My candours in palimpsest,
My collected blotting papers.

Or, at a pinch, I could have
Implied in reduced haiku
A world of suffering, swaddled
In white silence like babies
The rows of words, the mono-
Syllabic titles – my brain sore
And, as I struggled to master
The colon, my poet's tongue
Scorched by nicotine and coffee,
By the voracious acids
Of my *Ars Poetica*,
My clenched fist – towards midnight –
A paperweight on the language.

Or a species of skinny stanza
Might have materialised
In laborious versions
After the Finnish, for epigraph
The wry juxtaposing of
Wise-cracks by Groucho or Mae West
And the hushed hexameters
Of the right pastoral poet
From the Silver Age – Bacchylides
For instance – the breathings reversed,
The accents wrong mostly – proof,
If such were needed, of my humour
Among the big dictionaries.

These were my options, I say –
Night-lights, will-o'-the-wisps
Out of bog-holes and dark corners
Pointing towards the asylum
Where, for a quid of tobacco
Or a snatch of melody,
I might have cut off my head
In so many words – to borrow
A diagnosis of John Clare's –
Siphoning through the ears
Letters of the alphabet
And, with the vowels and consonants,
My life of make-believe.

IN MAYO

I

For her sake once again I disinter
Imagination like a brittle skull
From where the separating vertebrae
And scapulae litter a sandy wind,

As though to reach her I must circle
This burial mound, its shadow turning
Under the shadow of a seabird's wing:
A sundial for the unhallowed soul.

II

Though the townland's all ears, all eyes
To decipher our movements, she and I
Appear on the scene at the oddest times:
We follow the footprints of animals,

Then vanish into the old wives' tales
Leaving behind us landmarks to be named
After our episodes, and the mushrooms
That cluster where we happen to lie.

III

When it is time for her to fall asleep
And I touch her eyelids, may night itself,
By my rule of thumb, be no profounder
Than the grassy well among irises

Where wild duck shelter their candid eggs:
No more beguiling than a gull's feather
In whose manifold gradations of light
I clothe her now and erase the scene.

IV

Dawns and dusks here should consist of
Me scooping a hollow for her hip-bone,
The stony headland a bullaun, a cup
To balance her body in like water:

Then a slow awakening to the swans
That fly home in twos, married for life,
Larks nestling beside the cattle's feet
And snipe the weight of the human soul.

FLORA

A flutter of leaves
And pages open
Where, as my bookmark,
A flower is pressed,

Calyx, filament,
Anther staining
These pictures of me
In waste places

Shadowing sheep-tracks
From seacliff to dunes,
Ditches that drain
The salty marshes,

Naming the outcasts
Where petal and bud
Colour a runnel
Or sodden pasture,

Where bell and bugle,
A starry cluster
Or butterfly wing
Convey me farther

And in memory
And hands deposit
Blue periwinkles,
Meadowsweet, tansy.

LANDSCAPE

Here my imagination
Tangles through a turfstack
Like skeins of sheep's wool:
Is a bull's horn silting
With powdery seashells.

I am clothed, unclothed
By racing cloud shadows,
Or else disintegrate
Like a hillside neighbour
Erased by sea mist.

A place of dispersals
Where the wind fractures
Flight-feathers, insect wings
And rips thought to tatters
Like a fuchsia petal.

For seconds, dawn or dusk,
The sun's at an angle
To read inscriptions by:
The splay of the badger
And the otter's skidmarks

Melting into water
Where a minnow flashes:
A mouth drawn to a mouth
Digests the glass between
Me and my reflection.

POINTS OF THE COMPASS

for John Hewitt

Inscription

A stone inscribed with a cross,
The four points of the compass
Or a confluence of lines,
Crossroads and roundabout:
Someone's last milestone, propped
At an angle to the nettles,
A station that staggers still
Through tendrils of silverweed:
To understand what it says
I have cleared this area
Next to the casual arc
A thorn traces upon stone.

Clapper Bridge

One way to proceed:
Taking the water step
By step, stepping stones
With a roof over them,
A bed of standing stones,
Watery windows sunk
Into a dry-stone wall,
Porches for the water,
Some twists completing it
And these imperfections
Set, like the weather,
On the eve of mending.

Cell

After the entire structure
Has been sited thoughtfully
To straddle a mountain stream,
The ideal plan would include
A path leading from woodland,
From sorrel and watercress
To the one door, a window
Framing the salmon weir,
A hole for smoke, crevices
For beetles or saxifrage
And, for the fear of flooding,
Room enough under the floor.

Standing Stone

Where two lakes suggest petals
Of vetch or the violet,
The wings of a butterfly,
Ink blots reflecting the mind,
There, to keep them apart
As versions of each other,
To record the distances
Between islands of sunlight
And, as hub of the breezes,
To administer the scene
From its own peninsula,
A stone stands, a standing stone.

HALCYON

Grandmother's plumage was death
To the few remaining grebes,
The solitary kingfisher
That haunted a riverbank.

But, then, I consider her
The last of the Pearly Queens
To walk under tall feathers –
The trophies of sweethearts

Who aimed from leafy towpaths
Pistols, silver bullets,
Or sank among bullrushes
Laying out nets of silk.

So many trigger fingers
And hands laid upon water
Should let materialise
A bird that breeds in winter,

That settles bad weather,
The winds of sickness and death –
Halcyon to the ancients
And kingfisher in those days,

Though perhaps even she knew
It was the eccentric grebe
Whose feet covered the surface,
Whose nest floated on the waves.

MASTER OF CEREMONIES

My grandfather, a natural master of ceremonies,
('Boys! Girls! Take your partners for the Military Two-step!')
Had thrown out his only son, my sad retarded uncle
Who, good for nothing except sleepwalking to the Great War,
Was not once entrusted with rifle or bayonet but instead
Went over the top slowly behind the stretcher parties
And, as park attendant where all hell had broken loose,
Collected littered limbs until his sack was heavy.
In old age my grandfather demoted his flesh and blood
And over the cribbage board ('Fifteen two, fifteen four,
One for his nob') would call me Lionel. 'Sorry. My mistake.
That was my nephew. His head got blown off in No Man's Land.'

EDWARD THOMAS'S WAR DIARY

1 January – 8 April, 1917

One night in the trenches
You dreamed you were at home
And couldn't stay to tea,
Then woke where shell holes
Filled with bloodstained water,

Where empty beer bottles
Littered the barbed wire – still
Wondering why there sang
No thrushes in all that
Hazel, ash and dogwood,

Your eye on what remained –
Light spangling through a hole
In the cathedral wall
And the little conical
Summer house among trees.

Green feathers of yarrow
Were just fledging the sods
Of your dugout when you
Skirted the danger zone
To draw panoramas,

To receive larks singing
Like a letter from home
Posted in No Man's Land
Where one frantic bat seemed
A piece of burnt paper.

FLEANCE

I entered with a torch before me
And cast my shadow on the backcloth
Momentarily: a handful of words,
One bullet with my initials on it –
And that got stuck in a property tree.

I would have caught it between my teeth
Or, a true professional, stood still
While the two poetic murderers
Pinned my silhouette to history
In a shower of accurate daggers.

But as any illusionist might
Unfasten the big sack of darkness,
The ropes and handcuffs, and emerge
Smoking a nonchalant cigarette,
I escaped – only to lose myself.

It took me a lifetime to explore
The dusty warren beneath the stage
With its trapdoor opening on to
All that had happened above my head
Like noises-off or distant weather.

In the empty auditorium I bowed
To one preoccupied caretaker
And, without removing my make-up,
Hurried back to the digs where Banquo
Sat up late with a hole in his head.

COMPANY

I imagine a day when the children
Are drawers full of soft toys, photographs
Beside the only surviving copies
Of the books that summarise my lifetime,
And I have begun to look forward to
Retirement, second childhood, except that
Love has diminished to one high room
Below which the vigilantes patrol
While I attempt to make myself heard
Above the cacophonous plumbing, and you
Who are my solitary interpreter
Can bear my company for long enough
To lipread such fictions as I believe
Will placate remote customs officials,
The border guards, or even reassure
Anxious butchers, greengrocers, tradesmen
On whom we depend for our daily bread,
The dissemination of manuscripts,
News from the outside world, simple acts
Of such unpatriotic generosity
That until death we hesitate together
On the verge of an almost total silence:

Or else we are living in the country
In a far-off townland divided by
The distances it takes to overhear
A quarrel or the sounds of love-making,
Where even impoverished households
Can afford to focus binoculars
On our tiny windows, the curtains
That wear my motionless silhouette
As I sit late beside a tilley-lamp
And try to put their district on the map

And to name the fields for them, for you
Who busy yourself about the cottage,
Its thatch letting in, the tall grasses
And the rain leaning against the half-door,
Dust on the rafters and our collection
Of curious utensils, pots and pans
The only escape from which is the twice
Daily embarrassed journey to and from
The well we have choked with alder branches
For the cattle's safety, their hoofprints
A thirsty circle in the puddles,
Watermarks under all that we say.

MAN LYING ON A WALL

Homage to L. S. Lowry

You could draw a straight line from the heels,
Through calves, buttocks and shoulderblades
To the back of the head: pressure points
That bear the enormous weight of the sky.
Should you take away the supporting structure
The result would be a miracle or
An extremely clever conjuring trick.
As it is, the man lying on the wall
Is wearing the serious expression
Of popes and kings in their final slumber,
His deportment not dissimilar to
Their stiff, reluctant exits from this world
Above the shoulders of the multitude.

It is difficult to judge whether or not
He is sleeping or merely disinclined
To arrive punctually at the office
Or to return home in time for his tea.
He is wearing a pinstripe suit, black shoes
And a bowler hat: on the pavement
Below him, like a relic or something
He is trying to forget, his briefcase
With everybody's initials on it.

OBSEQUIES

They are proof-reading my obituary now
As I fall asleep in formalin and float
Just below the surface of death, mute
At the centre of my long obsequies.

Were they to queue up to hear me breathing
The chemicals, then head over heels
All my lovers would fall in love again,
For I am a big fish in the aquarium,

A saint whose bits and pieces separate
Into a dozen ceremonies, pyres
For hands that bedded down like Gandhi
With the untouchables, funerals for feet.

They have set my eyes like two diamonds
In the black velvet of another's head,
Bartered silver, gold from knuckle and tooth
To purchase some sustenance for the needy.

Meanwhile, back at the dissecting theatre,
Part of me waits to find in sinks and basins
A final ocean, tears, water from the tap,
Superstitious rivers to take me there.

WREATHS

The Civil Servant

He was preparing an Ulster fry for breakfast
When someone walked into the kitchen and shot him:
A bullet entered his mouth and pierced his skull,
The books he had read, the music he could play.

He lay in his dressing gown and pyjamas
While they dusted the dresser for fingerprints
And then shuffled backwards across the garden
With notebooks, cameras and measuring tapes.

They rolled him up like a red carpet and left
Only a bullet hole in the cutlery drawer:
Later his widow took a hammer and chisel
And removed the black keys from his piano.

The Greengrocer

He ran a good shop, and he died
Serving even the death-dealers
Who found him busy as usual
Behind the counter, organised
With holly wreaths for Christmas,
Fir trees on the pavement outside.

Astrologers or three wise men
Who may shortly be setting out
For a small house up the Shankill
Or the Falls, should pause on their way
To buy gifts at Jim Gibson's shop,
Dates and chestnuts and tangerines.

The Linen Workers

Christ's teeth ascended with him into heaven:
Through a cavity in one of his molars
The wind whistles: he is fastened for ever
By his exposed canines to a wintry sky.

I am blinded by the blaze of that smile
And by the memory of my father's false teeth
Brimming in their tumbler: they wore bubbles
And, outside of his body, a deadly grin.

When they masscred the ten linen workers
There fell on the road beside them spectacles,
Wallets, small change, and a set of dentures:
Blood, food particles, the bread, the wine.

Before I can bury my father once again
I must polish the spectacles, balance them
Upon his nose, fill his pockets with money
And into his dead mouth slip the set of teeth.

SECOND SIGHT

My father's mother had the second sight.
Flanders began at the kitchen window –
The mangle rusting in No Man's Land, gas
Turning the antimacassars yellow
When it blew the wrong way from the salient.

In bandages, on crutches, reaching home
Before his letters, my father used to find
The front door on the latch, his bed airing.
'I watched my son going over the top.
He was carrying flowers out of the smoke.'

I have brought the *Pocket Guide to London*,
My *Map of the Underground*, an address –
A lover looking for somewhere to live,
A ghost among ghosts of aunts and uncles
Who crowd around me to give directions.

Where is my father's house, where my father?
If I could walk in on my grandmother
She'd see right through me and the hallway
And the miles of cloud and sky to Ireland.
'You have crossed the water to visit me.'

ASH KEYS

Ghosts of hedgers and ditchers,
The ash trees rattling keys
Above tangles of hawthorn
And bramble, alder and gorse,

Would keep me from pacing
Commonage, long perspectives
And conversations, a field
That touches the horizon.

I am herding cattle there
As a boy, as the old man
Following in his footsteps
Who begins the task again,

As though there'd never been
In some interim or hollow
Wives and children, milk
And buttermilk, market days.

Far from the perimeter
Of watercress and berries,
In the middle of the field
I stand talking to myself,

While the ash keys scatter
And the gates creak open
And the barbed wire rusts
To hay-ropes strung with thorns.

SPRING TIDE

I

I seem lower than the distant waves,
Their roar diluting to the stillness
Of the sea's progression across these flats,
A map of water so adjusted
It behaves like a preservative
And erases neither the cattle's
And the sheep's nor my own footprints.
I leave hieroglyphics under glass
As well as feathers that hardly budge,
Down abandoned at preening places
That last so long as grassy islands
Where swans unravel among the ferns.

II

It isn't really a burial mound
Reflected there, but all that remains
Of a sandy meadow, a graveyard
Where it was easy to dig the graves.
The spring tide circles and excavates
A shrunken ramshackle pyramid
Rinsing cleaner scapulae, tibias,
Loose teeth, cowrie and nautilus shells
Before seeping after sun and moon
To pour cupfuls into the larks' nests,
To break a mirror on the grazing
And lift minnows over the low bridge.

III

The spring tide has ferried jellyfish
To the end of the lane, pinks, purples,
Wet flowers beside the floating cow-pats.
The zig-zags I make take me among
White cresses and brookweed, lousewort,
Water plantain and grass of parnassus
With engraved capillaries, ivory sheen:
By a dry-stone wall in the dune slack
The greenish sepals, the hidden blush
And a lip's red veins and yellow spots –
Marsh helleborine waiting for me
To come and go with the spring tide.

FROZEN RAIN

I slow down the waterfall to a chandelier,
Filaments of daylight, bones fleshed out by ice
That recuperate in their bandages of glass
And, where the lake behaves like a spirit-level,
I save pockets of air for the otter to breathe.

I magnify each individual blade of grass
With frozen rain, a crop of icicles and twigs,
Fingers and thumbs that beckon towards the thaw
And melt to the marrow between lip and tongue
While the wind strikes the branches like a celeste.

THAW

Snow curls into the coalhouse, flecks the coal.
We burn the snow as well in bad weather
As though to spring-clean that darkening hole.
The thaw's a blackbird with one white feather.

from MAYO MONOLOGUES

Brothers

I was a mother and a father to him
Once his pebble spectacles had turned cloudy
And his walk slowed to a chair by the fire.
Often I would come back from herding sheep
Or from the post office with our pensions
To find his darkness in darkness, the turf
Shifting ashes on to last flakes of light.
The room was made more silent by the flies
That circled the soup stains on his waistcoat.
The dog preferred to curl up under his hand
And raced ahead as soon as I neared the lane.
I read to him from one of his six books,
Thick pages dropping from the broken spines
Of *Westward Ho!* and *The Children's Reciter*.
Sometimes I pulled faces, and he didn't know,
Or I paraded naked in front of him
As though I was looking in a mirror.
Two neighbours came visiting after he died.
Mad for the learning, a character, they said
And awakened in me a pride of sorts.
I picture his hand when I stroke the dog,
His legs if I knock the kettle from the hearth.
It's his peculiar way of putting things
That fills in the spaces of Thallabaun.
The dregs stewed in the teapot remind me,
And wind creaming rainwater off the butt.

Self-heal

I wanted to teach him the names of flowers,
Self-heal and centaury; on the long acre
Where cattle never graze, bog asphodel.
Could I love someone so gone in the head
And, as they say, was I leading him on?
He'd slept in the cot until he was twelve
Because of his babyish ways, I suppose,
Or the lack of a bed: hadn't his father
Gambled away all but rushy pasture?
His skull seemed to be hammered like a wedge
Into his shoulders, and his back was hunched,
Which gave him an almost scholarly air.
But he couldn't remember the things I taught:
Each name would hover above its flower
Like a butterfly unable to alight.
That day I pulled a cuckoo-pint apart
To release the giddy insects from their cell.
Gently he slipped his hand between my thighs.
I wasn't frightened; and still I don't know why,
But I ran from him in tears to tell them.
I heard how every day for one whole week
He was flogged with a blackthorn, then tethered
In the hayfield. I might have been the cow
Whose tail he would later dock with shears,
And he the ram tangled in barbed wire
That he stoned to death when they set him free.

BOG COTTON

Let me make room for bog cotton, a desert flower –
Keith Douglas, I nearly repeat what you were saying
When you apostrophised the poppies of Flanders
And the death of poetry there: that was in Egypt
Among the sandy soldiers of another war.

(It hangs on by a thread, denser than thistledown,
Reluctant to fly, a weather vane that traces
The flow of cloud shadow over monotonous bog –
And useless too, though it might well bring to mind
The plumpness of pillows, the staunching of wounds,

Rags torn from a petticoat and soaked in water
And tied to the bushes around some holy well
As though to make a hospital of the landscape –
Cures and medicines as far as the horizon
Which nobody harvests except with the eye.)

You saw that beyond the thirstier desert flowers
There fell hundreds of thousands of poppy petals
Magnified to blood stains by the middle distance
Or through the still unfocused sights of a rifle –
And Isaac Rosenberg wore one behind his ear.

THE WAR POETS

Unmarked were the bodies of the soldier-poets
For shrapnel opened up again the fontanel
Like a hailstone melting towards deep water
At the bottom of a well, or a mosquito
Balancing its tiny shadow above the lip.

It was rushes of air that took the breath away
As though curtains were drawn suddenly aside
And darkness streamed into the dormitory
Where everybody talked about the war ending
And always it would be the last week of the war.

PEACE
after Tibullus

Who was responsible for the very first arms deal –
The man of iron who thought of marketing the sword?
Or did he intend us to use it against wild animals
Rather than ourselves? Even if he's not guilty
Murder got into the bloodstream as gene or virus
So that now we give birth to wars, short cuts to death.
Blame the affluent society: no killings when
The cup on the dinner table was made of beechwood,
And no barricades or ghettos when the shepherd
Snoozed among sheep that weren't even thoroughbreds.

I would like to have been alive in the good old days
Before the horrors of modern warfare and warcries
Stepping up my pulse rate. Alas, as things turn out
I've been press-ganged into service, and for all I know
Someone's polishing a spear with my number on it.
God of my Fathers, look after me like a child!
And don't be embarrassed by this handmade statue
Carved out of bog oak by my great-great-grandfather
Before the mass-production of religious art
When a wooden god stood simply in a narrow shrine.

A man could worship there with bunches of early grapes,
A wreath of whiskery wheat-ears, and then say Thank you
With a wholemeal loaf delivered by him in person,
His daughter carrying the unbroken honeycomb.
If the good Lord keeps me out of the firing line
I'll pick a porker from the steamy sty and dress
In my Sunday best, a country cousin's sacrifice.
Someone else can slaughter enemy commanders
And, over a drink, rehearse with me his memoirs,
Mapping the camp in wine upon the table top.

It's crazy to beg black death to join the ranks
Who dogs our footsteps anyhow with silent feet –
No cornfields in Hell, nor cultivated vineyards,
Only yapping Cerberus and the unattractive
Oarsman of the Styx: there an anaemic crew
Sleepwalks with smoky hair and empty eye-sockets.
How much nicer to have a family and let
Lazy old age catch up on you in your retirement,
You keeping track of the sheep, your son of the lambs,
While the woman of the house puts on the kettle.

I want to live until the white hairs shine above
A pensioner's memories of better days. Meanwhile
I would like peace to be my partner on the farm,
Peace personified: oxen under the curved yoke;
Compost for the vines, grape-juice turning into wine,
Vintage years handed down from father to son;
Hoe and ploughshare gleaming, while in some dark corner
Rust keeps the soldier's grisly weapons in their place;
The labourer steering his wife and children home
In a hay cart from the fields, a trifle sozzled.

Then, if there are skirmishes, guerilla tactics,
It's only lovers quarrelling, the bedroom door
Wrenched off its hinges, a woman in hysterics,
Hair torn out, cheeks swollen with bruises and tears –
Until the bully-boy starts snivelling as well
In a pang of conscience for his battered wife:
Then sexual neurosis works them up again
And the row escalates into a war of words.
He's hard as nails, made of sticks and stones, the chap
Who beats his girlfriend up. A crime against nature.

Enough, surely, to rip from her skin the flimsiest
Of negligees, ruffle that elaborate hair-do,
Enough to be the involuntary cause of tears –
Though upsetting a sensitive girl when you sulk
Is a peculiar satisfaction. But punch-ups,
Physical violence, are out: you might as well
Pack your kit-bag, goose-step a thousand miles away
From the female sex. As for me, I want a woman
To come and fondle my ears of wheat and let apples
Overflow between her breasts. I shall call her Peace.

SULPICIA

Round this particular date I have drawn a circle
For Mars, dressed myself up for him, dressed to kill:
When I let my hair down I am a sheaf of wheat
And I bring in the harvest without cutting it.

Were he to hover above me like a bird of prey
I would lay my body out, his little country,
Fields smelling of flowers, flowers in the hedgerow –
And then I would put on an overcoat of snow.

I will stumble behind him through the undergrowth
Tracking his white legs, drawing about us both
The hunters' circle: among twisted nets and snares

I will seduce him, tangle his hairs with my hairs
While the stag dashes off on one of its tangents
And boars root safely along our circumference.

GRACE DARLING

After you had steered your coble out of the storm
And left the smaller islands to break the surface,
Like draughts shaking that colossal backcloth there came
Fifty pounds from the Queen, proposals of marriage.

The daughter of a lighthouse-keeper and the saints
Who once lived there on birds' eggs, rainwater, barley
And built to keep all pilgrims at a safe distance
Circular houses with views only of the sky,

Who set timber burning on the top of a tower
Before each was launched at last in his stone coffin –
You would turn your back on mainland and suitor
To marry, then bereave the waves from Lindisfarne,

A moth against the lamp that shines still and reveals
Many small boats at sea, lifeboats, named after girls.

ON MWEELREA

I

I was lowering my body on to yours
When I put my ear to the mountain's side
And eavesdropped on water washing itself
In the locked bath-house of the underground.

When I dipped my hand among hidden sounds
It was the water's pulse at wrist and groin,
It was the water that reminded me
To leave all of my jugs and cups behind.

II

The slopes of the mountain were commonage
For me clambering over the low walls
To look for the rings of autumn mushrooms
That ripple out across the centuries.

I had made myself the worried shepherd
Of snipe twisting the grasses into curls
And tiny thatches where they hid away,
Of the sheep that grazed your maidenhair.

III

September grew to shadows on Mweelrea
Once the lambs had descended from the ridge
With their fleeces dyed, tinges of sunset,
Rowan berries, and the bracken rusting.

Behind my eyelids I could just make out
In a wash of blood and light and water
Your body colouring the mountainside
Like uncut poppies in the stubbly fields.

THE LINEN INDUSTRY

Pulling up flax after the blue flowers have fallen
And laying our handfuls in the peaty water
To rot those grasses to the bone, or building stooks
That recall the skirts of an invisible dancer,

We become a part of the linen industry
And follow its processes to the grubby town
Where fields are compacted into window-boxes
And there is little room among the big machines.

But even in our attic under the skylight
We make love on a bleach green, the whole meadow
Draped with material turning white in the sun
As though snow reluctant to melt were our attire.

What's passion but a battering of stubborn stalks,
Then a gentle combing out of fibres like hair
And a weaving of these into christening robes,
Into garments for a marriage or funeral?

Since it's like a bereavement once the labour's done
To find ourselves last workers in a dying trade,
Let flax be our matchmaker, our undertaker,
The provider of sheets for whatever the bed –

And be shy of your breasts in the presence of death,
Say that you look more beautiful in linen
Wearing white petticoats, the bow on your bodice
A butterfly attending the embroidered flowers.

SELF-PORTRAIT

My great-great-grandfather fell in top hat and tails
Across the threshold, his cigar brightly burning
While the chalk outline they had traced around his body
Got up and strolled through the door and became me,

But not before his own son had wasted a lifetime
Waiting to be made Lord Mayor of the Universe.
He was to choke to death on a difficult word
When a food particle lodged against his uvula.

I came into being alongside a twin brother
Who threatened me at first like an abortionist
Recommending suicide jumps and gin with cloves.
Then he blossomed into my guardian angel.

Peering back to the people who ploughed the Long Field
My eyes are bog holes that reflect a foreign sky.
Moustaches thatch my utterance in such a way
That no one can lipread the words from a distance.

I am, you will have noticed, all fingers and thumbs
But, then, so is the wing of a bat, a bird's wing.
I articulate through the nightingale's throat,
Sing with the vocal chords of the orang-outang.

PATCHWORK

I

There are ribbons that hold you together,
Hooks and eyes, hollows at the collarbone,

As though you dismantle your skeleton
Before stepping out of the crumpled ring,

Your nipples under my fingertips
Like white flowers on a white ground.

II

I pull up over us old clothes, remnants,
Stitching together shirts and nightshirts

Into such a dazzle as will burn away
Newspapers, letters, previous templates,

The hearth too, a red patch at the centre
That scorches the walls and our low ceiling.

MAGGIE MOORE'S

I am standing behind you in Maggie Moore's
Second-hand clothes shop in Sandy Row.
A single electric light bulb
Raises the bumps on the bumpy floor.
You rummage through crochet-work and cobwebs.

Moths flit out from the sweaty arm-holes
Of party frocks and summer dresses,
Nightdresses mothers and grandmothers wore.
As in a dream all take off their clothes
And vanish for ever down Sandy Row.

I am the guard who polishes his rifle
With a rag you recognise as silk
Or chiffon, perfect material
For you to embroider with designs
That cover and reveal your body.

And I am the young amazed GI
Passing rag after rag through barbed wire
And ripping the sleeve of his uniform.
He knows that your clothes are second-hand.
He brings down the shutters on Maggie Moore's.

LOVE POET

I make my peace with murderers.
I lock pubic hair from victims
In an airtight tin, mummify
Angel feathers, tobacco shreds.

All that survives my acid bath
Is a solitary gall-stone
Like a pebble out on mud flats
Or the ghost of an avocado.

HALLOWE'EN

It is Hallowe'en. Turnip Head
Will soon be given his face,
A slit, two triangles, a hole.
His brains litter the table top.
A candle stub will be his soul.

ON SLIEVE GULLION

for Douglas Carson

On Slieve Gullion 'men and mountain meet',
O'Hanlon's territory, the rapparee,
Home of gods, backdrop for a cattle raid,
The Lake of Cailleach Beara at the top
That slaked the severed head of Conor Mor:

To the south the Border and Ravensdale
Where the torturers of Nairac left
Not even an eyelash under the leaves
Or a tooth for MacCecht the cupbearer
To rinse, then wonder where the water went.

I watch now through a gap in the hazels
A blackened face, the disembodied head
Of a mummer who has lost his bearings
Or, from the garrison at Dromintee,
A paratrooper on reconnaissance.

He draws a helicopter after him,
His beret far below, a wine-red spot
Swallowed by heathery patches and ling
As he sweats up the slopes of Slieve Gullion
With forty pounds of history on his back.

Both strangers here, we pass in silence
For he and I have dried the lakes and streams
And Conor said too long ago: 'Noble
And valiant is MacCecht the cupbearer
Who brings water that a king may drink.'

SMOKE IN THE BRANCHES

The Disfigurement of Fergus

This is a scream no one will have heard
Bubbling up out of his mind, nightmare
Distorting his face on the sea-bed
To an ugliness that craves its mirror,
A watery death to cure and wash
The King of Ulster and his blemish.

The Grey of Macha

When big tears of blood roll down the face
Of the Grey of Macha, Cuchulain's horse,
They sprinkle the chariot and harness
That might as well be dragging a hearse
Over a battlefield slushy with brains,
Over the teeth like a shower of hailstones.

The Bewilderment of Muircertach

Muircertach mac Erca, King of Ireland,
Is waging war against fern and thistle,
Damaging pebbles, wounding the ground
Between life and death, grave and castle,
Where the woman he adores will vanish
Like a puff ball or smoke in the branches.

The Death of Mac Glas

He isn't pulling a funny face
Although the Leinstermen laugh at him
Who, seconds ago, was only Mac Glas
The jester contriving another game,
While the entrails, tugged by a raven
Out of his wound, loop up to heaven.

MARKINGS

for Sarah

I

The markings almost disappear
With the shadowy sound you make
Launching the feather from your hand,
As though you would learn to whistle
By answering the curlew's cry.

II

I would remember tumblers
Above the water-meadow,
The shimmer of white feathers
In the flower-dwarfing wind,

Brood-patch and bird-brain,
The hummock of her body
That tries to make head or tail
Of movements inside the shell.

All that remains to show you
Is the deserted nest-bowl,
Blots and scribbles on an egg,
The dappled flight of lapwings.

III

One more pebble on the cairn
Might make it a vantage point
For the stonechat, a headstone
Should winter blow out his song,
His chestnut breast a tinderbox
Igniting the few syllables.

THE WHITE BUTTERFLY

I wish that before you died
I had told you the legend,
A story from the Blaskets
About how the cabbage-white
May become the soul of one
Who lies sleeping in the fields.

Out of his mouth it wanders
And in through the eye-socket
Of an old horse's skull
To explore the corridors
And empty chamber, then
Flies back inside his lips.

This is a dream and flowers
Are bordering the journey
And the road leads on towards
That incandescent palace
Where from one room to the next
There is no one to be seen.

When I asked you as a child
How high should fences be
To keep in the butterflies,
Blood was already passing
Down median and margin
To the apex of a wing.

SEA SHANTY

I would have waited under the statue of Eros
While the wind whistled in my bell-bottoms,
Taken my bearings from the blink of daylight
Her thighs and feathery maidenhair let through.
But now from the high ground of Carrigskeewaun
I watch Lesbos rising among the islands.
Rain shivers off the machair, and exposes me
In my long-johns, who dozed on her breastbone,
On pillows of sea-pink beyond the shingle,
Who mumbled into the ringlets at her ear
My repertoire of sea shanties and love songs.
I shake like a rock-fern, and my ill will
And smoky breath seem to wither the lichens.
I am making do with what has been left me,
The saltier leaves of samphire for my salad.
At midnight the moon goes, then the Pleiades,
A sparkle of sand grains on my wellingtons.

BETWEEN HOVERS

in memory of Joe O'Toole

And not even when we ran over the badger
Did he tell me he had cancer, Joe O'Toole
Who was psychic about carburettor and clutch
And knew a folk cure for the starter-engine.
Backing into the dark we floodlit each hair
Like a filament of light our lights had put out
Somewhere between Kinnadoohy and Thallabaun.
I dragged it by two gritty paws into the ditch.
Joe spotted a ruby where the canines touched.
His way of seeing me safely across the duach
Was to leave his porch light burning, its sparkle
Shifting from widgeon to teal on Corragaun Lake.
I missed his funeral. Close to the stony roads
He lies in Killeen Churchyard over the hill.
This morning on the burial mound at Templedoomore
Encircled by a spring tide and taking in
Cloonaghmanagh and Claggan and Carrigskeewaun,
The townlands he'd wandered tending cows and sheep,
I watched a dying otter gaze right through me
At the islands in Clew Bay, as though it were only
Between hovers and not too far from the holt.

DETOUR

I want my funeral to include this detour
Down the single street of a small market town,
On either side of the procession such names
As Philbin, O'Malley, MacNamara, Keane.
A reverent pause to let a herd of milkers pass
Will bring me face to face with grubby parsnips,
Cauliflowers that glitter after a sunshower,
Then hay rakes, broom handles, gas cylinders.
Reflected in the slow sequence of shop windows
I shall be part of the action when his wife
Draining the potatoes into a steamy sink
Calls to the butcher to get ready for dinner
And the publican descends to change a barrel.
From behind the one locked door for miles around
I shall prolong a detailed conversation
With the man in the concrete telephone kiosk
About where my funeral might be going next.

GORSE FIRES

Cattle out of their byres are dungy still, lambs
Have stepped from last year as from an enclosure.
Five or six men stand gazing at a rusty tractor
Before carrying implements to separate fields.

I am travelling from one April to another.
It is the same train between the same embankments.
Gorse fires are smoking, but primroses burn
And celandines and white may and gorse flowers.

REMEMBERING CARRIGSKEEWAUN

A wintry night, the hearth inhales
And the chimney becomes a windpipe
Fluffy with soot and thistledown,
A voice-box recalling animals:
The leveret come of age, snipe
At an angle, then the porpoises'
Demonstration of meaningless smiles.
Home is a hollow between the waves,
A clump of nettles, feathery winds,
And memory no longer than a day
When the animals come back to me
From the townland of Carrigskeewaun,
From a page lit by the Milky Way.

HOMECOMING

The brightest star came out, the day-star, dawn's star
And the seafaring ship drew near to Ithaca, to home
And that harbour named after the old man of the sea, two
Headlands huddling together as breakwater, windbreak,
Haven where complicated vessels float free of moorings
In their actual mooring-places.
                                                At the harbour-head
A long-leaved olive overshadows a shadowy cave
Full of bullauns, basins hollowed out of stone, stone
Jars for honey-bees, looms of stone on which are woven
Sea-purplish things – also, inextinguishable springs
And two ways in, one looking north where men descend
While the other faces south, a footpath for the gods.

When they had scrunched ashore at this familiar cove
And disembarked, they lifted Odysseus out of his hollow
Just as he was, linen sheet and glossy rug and all,
And put him to bed on the sand, still lost in sleep.

AN AMISH RUG

As if a one-room schoolhouse were all we knew
And our clothes were black, our underclothes black,
Marriage a horse and buggy going to church
And the children silhouettes in a snowy field,

I bring you this patchwork like a smallholding
Where I served as the hired boy behind the harrow,
Its threads the colour of cantaloupe and cherry
Securing hay bales, corn cobs, tobacco leaves.

You may hang it on the wall, a cathedral window,
Or lay it out on the floor beside our bed
So that whenever we undress for sleep or love
We shall step over it as over a flowerbed.

COUCHETTE

With my wife, son, daughter in layers up the walls
This room on wheels has become the family vault.
They have fallen asleep, dreams stopping and starting
As my long coffin wobbles on the top couchette.
Shunted down a siding, we shall wait for centuries
Before hurtling to places we have never seen.
No more than a blink of light, a tinkle of bangles,
The old woman who joins us at Turin will leave
Crusts and a plastic bottle of mineral water.
Soon her space will be taken by a younger lady
We met four thousand years ago in Fiesole,
Her face still to be uncovered, and at her feet
A pet cat who has also been wrapped in bandages.

LAERTES

When he found Laertes alone on the tidy terrace, hoeing
Around a vine, disreputable in his gardening duds,
Patched and grubby, leather gaiters protecting his shins
Against brambles, gloves as well, and, to cap it all,
Sure sign of his deep depression, a goatskin duncher,
Odysseus sobbed in the shade of a pear-tree for his father
So old and pathetic that all he wanted then and there
Was to kiss him and hug him and blurt out the whole story,
But the whole story is one catalogue and then another,
So he waited for images from that formal garden,
Evidence of a childhood spent traipsing after his father
And asking for everything he saw, the thirteen pear-trees,
Ten apple-trees, forty fig-trees, the fifty rows of vines
Ripening at different times for a continuous supply,
Until Laertes recognised his son and, weak at the knees,
Dizzy, flung his arms around the neck of great Odysseus
Who drew the old man fainting to his breast and held him there
And cradled like driftwood the bones of his dwindling father.

ANTICLEIA

If at a rock where the resonant rivers meet, Acheron,
Pyriphlegethon, Cocytus, tributary of the Styx, you dig
A pit, about a cubit each way, from knuckles to elbow,
And sacrifice a ram and a black ewe, bending their heads
Towards the outer darkness, while you face the water,
And so many souls of the anaemic dead come crowding in
That you hold them back with your bayonet from the blood
Only to recognise among the zombies your own mother,
And if, having given her blood to drink and talked about home,
You lunge forward three times to hug her and three times
Like a shadow or idea she vanishes through your arms
And you ask her why she keeps avoiding your touch and weep
Because here is your mother and even here in Hades
You could comfort each other in a shuddering embrace,
Will she explain that the sinews no longer bind her flesh
And bones, that the irresistible fire has demolished these,
That the soul takes flight like a dream and flutters in the sky,
That this is what happens to human beings when they die?

TEREZÍN

No room has ever been as silent as the room
Where hundreds of violins are hung in unison.

GHETTO

I

Because you will suffer soon and die, your choices
Are neither right nor wrong: a spoon will feed you,
A flannel keep you clean, a toothbrush bring you back
To your bathroom's view of chimney-pots and gardens.
With so little time for inventory or leavetaking,
You are packing now for the rest of your life
Photographs, medicines, a change of underwear, a book,
A candlestick, a loaf, sardines, needle and thread.
These are your heirlooms, perishables, wordly goods.
What you bring is the same as what you leave behind,
Your last belonging a list of your belongings.

II

As though it were against the law to sleep on pillows
They have filled a cathedral with confiscated feathers:
Silence irrefrangible, no room for angels' wings,
Tons of feathers suffocating cherubim and seraphim.

III

The little girl without a mother behaves like a mother
With her rag doll to whom she explains fear and anguish,
The meagreness of the bread ration, how to make it last,
How to get back to the doll's house and lift up the roof
And, before the flame-throwers and dynamiters destroy it,
How to rescue from their separate rooms love and sorrow,
Masterpieces the size of a postage stamp, small fortunes.

IV

From among the hundreds of thousands I can imagine one
Behind the barbed-wire fences as my train crosses Poland.
I see him for long enough to catch the sprinkle of snowflakes
On his hair and schoolbag, and then I am transported
Away from that world of broken hobby-horses and silent toys.
He turns into a little snowman and refuses to melt.

V

For street-singers in the marketplace, weavers, warp-makers,
Those who suffer in sewing-machine repair shops, excrement-
Removal workers, there are not enough root vegetables,
Beetroots, turnips, swedes, nor for the leather-stitchers
Who are boiling leather so that their children may eat;
Who are turning like a thick slice of potato-bread
This page, which is everything I know about potatoes,
My delivery of Irish Peace, Beauty of Hebron, Home
Guard, Arran Banners, Kerr's Pinks, resistant to eelworm,
Resignation, common scab, terror, frost, potato-blight.

VI

There will be performances in the waiting room, and time
To jump over a skipping rope, and time to adjust
As though for a dancing class the ribbons in your hair.
This string quartet is the most natural thing in the world.

VII

Fingers leave shadows on a violin, harmonics,
A blackbird fluttering between electrified fences.

VIII

Lessons were forbidden in that terrible school.
Punishable by death were reading and writing
And arithmetic, so that even the junior infants
Grew old and wise in lofts studying these subjects.
There were drawing lessons, and drawings of kitchens
And farms, farm animals, butterflies, mothers, fathers
Who survived in crayon until in pen and ink
They turned into guards at executions and funerals
Torturing and hanging even these stick figures.
There were drawings of barracks and latrines as well
And the only windows were the windows they drew.

ARGOS

There were other separations, and so many of them
That Argos the dog who waited twenty years for Odysseus
Has gone on waiting, still neglected on the manure-heap
At our front door, flea-ridden, more dead than alive
Who chased wild goats once, and roe-deer; the favourite,
A real thoroughbred, a marvel at picking up the scent,
Who even now is wagging his tail and drooping his ears
And struggling to get nearer to the voice he recognises
And dying in the attempt; until like Odysseus
We weep for Argos the dog, and for all those other dogs,
For the rounding-up of hamsters, the panic of white mice
And the deportation of one canary called Pepicek.

THE BUTCHERS

When he had made sure there were no survivors in his house
And that all the suitors were dead, heaped in blood and dust
Like fish that fishermen with fine-meshed nets have hauled
Up gasping for salt water, evaporating in the sunshine,
Odysseus, spattered with muck and like a lion dripping blood
From his chest and cheeks after devouring a farmer's bullock,
Ordered the disloyal housemaids to sponge down the armchairs
And tables, while Telemachos, the oxherd and the swineherd
Scraped the floor with shovels, and then between the portico
And the roundhouse stretched a hawser and hanged the women
So none touched the ground with her toes, like long-winged thrushes
Or doves trapped in a mist-net across the thicket where they roost,
Their heads bobbing in a row, their feet twitching but not for long,
And when they had dragged Melanthios's corpse into the haggard
And cut off his nose and ears and cock and balls, a dog's dinner,
Odysseus, seeing the need for whitewash and disinfectant,
Fumigated the house and the outhouses, so that Hermes
Like a clergyman might wave the supernatural baton
With which he resurrects or hypnotises those he chooses,
And waken and round up the suitors' souls, and the housemaids',
Like bats gibbering in the nooks of their mysterious cave
When out of the clusters that dangle from the rocky ceiling
One of them drops and squeaks, so their souls were bat-squeaks
As they flittered after Hermes, their deliverer, who led them
Along the clammy sheughs, then past the oceanic streams
And the white rock, the sun's gatepost in that dreamy region,
Until they came to a bog-meadow full of bog-asphodels
Where the residents are ghosts or images of the dead.

THE ICE-CREAM MAN

Rum and raisin, vanilla, butter-scotch, walnut, peach:
You would rhyme off the flavours. That was before
They murdered the ice-cream man on the Lisburn Road
And you bought carnations to lay outside his shop.
I named for you all the wild flowers of the Burren
I had seen in one day: thyme, valerian, loosestrife,
Meadowsweet, tway blade, crowfoot, ling, angelica,
Herb robert, marjoram, cow parsley, sundew, vetch,
Mountain avens, wood sage, ragged robin, stitchwort,
Yarrow, lady's bedstraw, bindweed, bog pimpernel.

PONIES

I

Carved out of the darkness and far below
In the very last working, a stable
Where the pressure transforms into trees
Pit-props, rosettes into sunflowers,
Into grazing nosebags and the droppings
That smoulder among lumps of coal.

II

Like the fuzzy star her forelock covers,
A yarn about a townland somewhere –
Two fields and no more, in one of them
The convergence of three counties, and her
Standing up to the gaskins in foxgloves,
Agrimony, swaying meadowsweet.

FORM

Trying to tell it all to you and cover everything
Is like awakening from its grassy form the hare:
In that make-shift shelter your hand, then my hand
Mislays the hare and the warmth it leaves behind.

AUTUMN LADY'S TRESSES

How does the solitary swan on Dooaghtry Lake
Who knows all about the otter as a glimmer
Among reeds, as water unravelling, as watery
Corridors into the water, a sudden face,
Receive through the huge silence of sand-dunes
Signals from the otters' rock at Allaran Point
About another otter, the same otter, folding
Sunlight into the combers like brown kelp,
Or the dolphins whose waves within waves propel
You and me along the strand like young lovers,
Or the aftermath of lit thistledown, peacock
Butterflies above marram grass, lady's tresses
That wind into their spirals of white flowers
Cowrie shells for decorating your sandy hair?

WATERCOLOUR

for Jeffrey Morgan

Between a chicken's wishbone on the mantelpiece
And, on the window sill, a dolphin's skull, I sit,
My pullover a continuation of the lazy-beds
You study through the window, my shirt a running
Together of earth-colours, wintry grasses, bracken
Painted with your favourite brush – goose-quill and sable
From a hundred years ago – and with water:
One drop too many and the whole thing disintegrates.
In this humidity your watercolour will never dry.

GRETTA BOWEN'S EMENDATIONS

Eighty when she first created pictures, Gretta Bowen
Postponed the finishing touches, and then in her nineties
Emended her world by painting on the glass that covered
Children's games, fairgrounds, swans on a pond, interiors
Not brush-strokes to erase her studious reflection
But additional leaves and feathers falling on to ice.

ACCORDING TO PYTHAGORAS

When in good time corpses go off and ooze in the heat
Creepy-crawlies breed in them. Bury your prize bull
(A well-known experiment) – and from the putrid guts
Swarm flower-crazy bees, industrious country-types
Working hard, as did their host, with harvest in mind.
An interred war-horse produces hornets. Remove
A shore-crab's hollow claw, lay it to rest: the result
Is a scorpion charging with its tail bent like a hook.
Worms cosy in cocoons of white thread grow into
Butterflies, souls of the dead. Any farmer knows that.

Germs in mud generate green frogs: legless at first
They soon sprout swimming and jumping equipment.
A she-bear's cub is a lump of meat whose stumpy
Non-legs she licks into shape in her own image.
The honey-bees' larvae hatched in those waxy hexagons
Only get feet and wings later on. That's obvious.
Think of peacocks, eagles, doves, the bird-family
As a whole, all starting inside eggs: hard to believe.
There's a theory that in the grave the backbone rots
Away and the spinal cord turns into a snake.

The fundamental interconnectedness of all things
Is incredible enough, but did you know that
Hyenas change sex? The female mounted by a male
Just minutes before, becomes a male herself. Then
There's the chameleon that feeds off wind and air
And takes the colour of whatever it's standing on.
Air transforms lynxes' urine into stones and hardens
Coral, that softly swaying underwater plant.
I could go on and on with these scientific facts.
If it wasn't so late I'd tell you a whole lot more.

SPIDERWOMAN

Arachne starts with Ovid and finishes with me.

Her hair falls out and the ears and nostrils disappear
From her contracting face, her body minuscule, thin
Fingers clinging to her sides by way of legs, the rest
All stomach, from which she manufactures gossamer
And so keeps up her former trade, weaver, spider

Enticing the eight eyes of my imagination
To make love on her lethal doily, to dangle sperm
Like teardrops from an eyelash, massage it into her
While I avoid the spinnerets – navel, vulva, bum –
And the widening smile behind her embroidery.

She wears our babies like brooches on her abdomen.

A FLOWERING

Now that my body grows woman-like I look at men
As two or three women have looked at me, then hide
Among Ovid's lovely casualties – all that blood
Colouring the grass and changing into flowers, purple,
Lily-shaped, wild hyacinth upon whose petals
We doodled our lugubrious initials, they and I,
Blood dosed with honey, tumescent, effervescent
– Clean bubbles in yellow mud – creating in an hour
My own son's beauty, the truthfulness of my nipples,
Petals that will not last long, that hang on and no more,
Youth and its flower named after the wind, anemone.

MR 10½
after Robert Mapplethorpe

When he lays out as on a market stall or altar
His penis and testicles in thanksgiving and for sale,
I find myself considering his first months in the womb
As a wee girl, and I substitute for his two plums
Plum-blossom, for his cucumber a yellowy flower.

MASSIVE LOVERS
after Katsushika Hokusai

I was the philosopher watching a pair of butterflies
Until massive lovers exposed my peedy and grey hairs –
His cock a gate-post, rain running off the glans, snow-broth
And the shriek of silk, hair-pins along the loney – and I
Became the pearl-diver hugged and sucked by octopuses.

A GRAIN OF RICE

Wrap my poem around your chopsticks to keep them clean.
I hardly know you. I do not want you to die. Our names
Fit on to a grain of rice like Hokusai's two sparrows,
Or else, like the praying mantis and the yellow butterfly,
We are a crowd in the garden where nothing grows but stones.
I do not understand the characters: sunlight through leaves,
An ivy pattern like fingers caressing a bowl, your face
In splinters where a carp kisses the moon, the waterfall
Up which its fins will spiral out of sight and into the sky.
Wrap my poem around your chopsticks to keep them clean.
Does it mean I shall not have taken one kiss for ever?
Your unimaginable breasts become the silk-worm's shrine.

CHINESE OBJECTS

I

The length of white silk I selected
Immaculate as the crust on snow
Was cut in the shape of happiness,
Round as the moon in starry skies.
In and out of her sleeve it slides
Rustling up its own cool weather.
I worry that when autumn comes
And blows away this heatwave,
She will toss the fan into a box
Half way through our love affair.

II

When the water-gourd that dangles
Light as a single leaf from the tree
Goes clickety-clack in the breeze
So that bed-sounds and love-making
Get into my dream, in my dream
I throw it away, for the world
Is not so big, the gourd so small:
They are objects outside my body
That get in the way of sleep.

THE SCISSORS CEREMONY

What they are doing makes their garden feel like a big room.
I spy on them through the hedge, through a hundred keyholes.
He sits in a deckchair. She leans over him from behind
As though he were a little boy, and clips his fingernails
Into the newspaper he balances between his knees. Her
White hair tickles his white hair. Her breath at his ear
Might be correcting his sums, disclosing the facts of life,
Recalling the other warm cheeks that have hesitated there.
He is not demented or lazy or incapacitated. No,
It is just that she enjoys clipping his fingernails
And scattering them like seeds out of a rattly packet.
Are they growing younger as I walk the length of the hedge?
Look! The scissors ceremony is a way of making love!

SNOW-HOLE

Falling asleep in the snowscape of the big double-bed
I wrap my hand around your hand until they catch fire
And the snow begins to melt and we sink down and down,
The fire and ourselves, how many feet below the morning.
Should our fingers burn out at the bottom of the snow-hole
Smoke will escape up the glass chimney into the bedroom.

THE EEL-TRAP

I lie awake and my mind goes out to the otter
That might be drowning in the eel-trap:
                                                            your breathing
Falters as I follow you to the other lake
Below sleep, the brown trout sipping at the stars.

PHOENIX

I'll hand to you six duck eggs Orla Murphy gave me
In a beechwood bowl Ted O'Driscoll turned, a nest
Jiggling eggs from Baltimore to Belfast, from friends
You haven't met, a double-yolk inside each shell
Laid by a duck that renovates and begets itself
Inside my head as the phoenix, without grass or corn,
On a strict diet of frankincense and cardamoms,
After five centuries builds with talons and clean beak
In the top branches of a quivering palm his nest,
Lining it with cassia, spikes of nard, cinnamon chips
And yellow myrrh, brooding among the spicy smells
His own death and giving birth to an only child
Who grows up to carry through thin air the heavy nest
– His cradle, his father's coffin – to the sun's city,
In front of the sun's doorway putting his bundle down
As I shall put down the eggs Orla Murphy gave me
In a beechwood bowl Ted O'Driscoll turned for her.

THE CAMP-FIRES

All night crackling camp-fires boosted their morale
As they dozed in no man's land and the killing fields.
(There are balmy nights – not a breath, constellations
Resplendent in the sky around a dazzling moon –
When a clearance high in the atmosphere unveils
The boundlessness of space, and all the stars are out
Lighting up hill-tops, glens, headlands, vantage
Points like Tonakeera and Allaran where the tide
Turns into Killary, where salmon run from the sea,
Where the shepherd smiles on his luminous townland.
That many camp-fires sparkled in front of Ilium
Between the river and the ships, a thousand fires,
Round each one fifty men relaxing in the fire-light.)
Shuffling next to the chariots, munching shiny oats
And barley, their horses waited for the sunrise.

THE HELMET

When shiny Hector reached out for his son, the wean
Squirmed and buried his head between his nurse's breasts
And howled, terrorised by his father, by flashing bronze
And the nightmarish nodding of the horse-hair crest.

His daddy laughed, his mammy laughed, and his daddy
Took off the helmet and laid it on the ground to gleam,
Then kissed the babbie and dandled him in his arms and
Prayed that his son might grow up bloodier than him.

POPPIES

I

Some people tried to stop other people wearing poppies
And ripped them from lapels as though uprooting poppies
From Flanders fields, but the others hid inside their poppies
Razor blades and added to their poppies more red poppies.

II

In Royal Avenue they tossed in the air with so much joy
Returning wounded soldiers, their stitches burst for joy.

CEASEFIRE

I

Put in mind of his own father and moved to tears
Achilles took him by the hand and pushed the old king
Gently away, but Priam curled up at his feet and
Wept with him until their sadness filled the building.

II

Taking Hector's corpse into his own hands Achilles
Made sure it was washed and, for the old king's sake,
Laid out in uniform, ready for Priam to carry
Wrapped like a present home to Troy at daybreak.

III

When they had eaten together, it pleased them both
To stare at each other's beauty as lovers might,
Achilles built like a god, Priam good-looking still
And full of conversation, who earlier had sighed:

IV

'I get down on my knees and do what must be done
And kiss Achilles' hand, the killer of my son.'

PHEMIOS & MEDON

Still looking for a scoot-hole, Phemios the poet
In swithers, fiddling with his harp, jukes to the hatch,
Lays the bruckle yoke between porringer and armchair,
Makes a ram-stam for Odysseus, grammels his knees,
Then bannies and bams wi this highfalutin blether:
'I ask for pity and respect. How could you condemn
A poet who writes for his people and Parnassus,
Autodidact, his repertoire god-given? I beg you
Not to be precipitate and cut off my head. Spare me
And I'll immortalise you in an ode. Telemachos
Your own dear son will vouch that I was no party-hack
At the suitors' dinner-parties. Overwhelmed and out-
Numbered, I gave poetry readings against my will.'
I gulder to me da: 'Dinnae gut him wi yer gully,
He's only a harmless crayter. And how's about Medon
The toast-master whose ashy-pet I was? Did ye ding him
When the oxherd and the swineherd stormed the steading?'
Thon oul gabble-blooter's a canny huer and hears me
From his fox's-slumber in cow-hides under a chair –
Out he spalters, flaffing his hands, blirting to my knees:
'Here I am, dear boy! Put in a word for me before
Your hot-blooded pater slaughters me as one of them –
The suitors I mean, bread-snappers, belly-bachelors.'
Long-headed Odysseus smiles at him and says: 'Wheesht!
You may thank Telemachos for this chance to wise up
And pass on the message of oul dacency. Go out
And sit in the haggard away from this massacre,
You and the well-spoken poet, while I redd the house.'
They hook it and hunker fornenst the altar of Zeus,
Afeard and skelly-eyed, keeking everywhere for death.

THE FISHING PARTY

Because he loves off-duty policemen and their murderers
Christ is still seen walking on the water of Lough Neagh,
Whose fingers created bluebottles, meadow-browns, red
Admirals, painted ladies, fire-flies, and are tying now
Woodcock hackles around hooks, lamb's wool, badger fur

Until about his head swarm artificial flies and their names,
Dark Mackerel, Gravel Bed, Greenwell's Glory, Soldier
Palmer, Coachman, Water Cricket, Orange Grouse, Barm,
Without snagging in his hair or ceasing to circle above
Policemen turned by gunmen into fishermen for ever.

BIRDSONG

'Where am I?' Consulting the *Modern School Atlas*
You underline Dalkey in Ireland, in Scotland Barrhead.
'What day is it?' Outside the home, house-sparrows
With precision tweetle and wheep under the eaves.

Although you forget their names, you hear the birds
In your own accent, the dawn chitter, evening chirl,
The woodpigeon's rooketty-coo and curdoo. 'Who
Am I? Where am I?' is what a bird might sing.

HEADSTONE

I

The headstone for my parents' grave in Drumbo churchyard
I have imagined only: a triangular slab from the spiral
Staircase in the round tower that nearly overshadows them,
A stumpy ruin beside which I have seen myself standing
And following everyone's forefinger up into the sky.

II

Because he had survived in a coracle made out of feathers
I want to ask him about the lock-keeper's house at Newforge
Where a hole grows in the water, and about the towpath
That follows the Styx as far as the Minnowburn Beeches
And the end of his dream, and about the oars like wings.

III

As though her ashes had been its cargo when the ice-boat
Was rocked at dawn like a cradle and hauled from Shaw's
Bridge past Drumbo and Drumbeg, all the way to Aghalee,
I can hear in the frosty air above Acheron ice cracking
And the clatter of horses' hooves on the slippery towpath.

IV

The wreck at Thallabaun whose timbers whistle in the wind
The tunes of shipwright, sawyer, cabinet-maker – adze
And axe and chisel following the grain – is my blue-print
For the ship of death, wood as hard as stone that keeps
Coming ashore with its cargo of sand and sandy water.

THE WHITE GARDEN

So white are the white flowers in the white garden that I
Disappear in no time at all among lace and veils.
For whom do I scribble the few words that come to me
From beyond the arch of white roses as from nowhere,
My memorandum to posterity? Listen. 'The saw
Is under the garden bench and the gate is unlatched.'

THE GHOST ORCHID

Added to its few remaining sites will be the stanza
I compose about leaves like flakes of skin, a colour
Dithering between pink and yellow, and then the root
That grows like coral among shadows and leaf-litter.
Just touching the petals bruises them into darkness.

CHINESE OCCASIONS

I

Snow piles up against the sunny window.
I burn my joss-sticks (a religious notion).
A blue tit tweetles from the patio.
The breeze sets a snowy twig in motion.

II

I am inspired by wind off the Lagan.
I tipple in the Black Mountain's shadow.
I fall into the flowerbed (drink taken),
Soil and sky my eiderdown and pillow.

III

They sip their whiskies on the patio.
Listen to them and what they listen to.
I close the door and open the window.
My friends grow feathers from top to toe.

IV

At the heart of the blue wisteria
A blackbird practises its aria.

RIVER & FOUNTAIN

I

I am walking backwards into the future like a Greek.
I have nothing to say. There is nothing I would describe.
It was always thus: as if snow has fallen on Front
Square, and, feeling the downy silence of the snowflakes
That cover cobbles and each other, white erasing white,
I read shadow and snow-drift under the Campanile.

II

'It fits on to the back of a postage stamp,' Robert said
As he scribbled out in tiny symbols the equation,
His silhouette a frost-flower on the window of my last
Year, his page the sky between chimney-stacks, his head
And my head at the city's centre aching for giddy
Limits, mathematics, poetry, squeaky nibs at all hours.

III

Top of the staircase, Number Sixteen in Botany Bay,
Slum-dwellers, we survived gas-rings that popped,
Slop-buckets in the bedrooms, changeable 'wives', and toasted
Doughy doorsteps, Freshmen turning into Sophisters
In front of the higgledy flames: our still-life, crusts
And buttery books, the half-empty marmalade jar.

IV

My Dansette record player bottled up like genies
Sibelius, Shostakovich, Bruckner, dusty sleeves
Accumulating next to Liddel and Scott's *Greek-English*
Lexicon voices the fluffy needle set almost free.
I was the culture vulture from Ulster, Vincent's joke
Who heard *The Rite of Spring* and contemplated suicide.

V

Adam was first to read the maroon-covered notebooks
I filled with innocent outpourings, Adam the scholar
Whose stammer could stop him christening this and that,
Whose Eden was annotation and vocabulary lists
In a precise classicist's hand, the love of words as words.
My first and best review was Adam's 'I like these – I – I –'

VI

'College poet? Village idiot you mean!' (Vincent again).
In neither profession could I settle comfortably
Once Derek arrived reciting Rimbaud, giving names
To the constellations over the Examination Hall.
'Are you Longley? Can I borrow your typewriter? Soon?'
His was the first snow party I attended. I felt the cold.

VII

We were from the North, hitch-hikers on the Newry Road,
Faces that vanished from a hundred driving-mirrors
Down that warren of reflections – O'Neill's Bar, Nesbitt's –
And through Front Gate to Connemara and Inisheer,
The raw experience of market towns and clachans, then
Back to Rooms, village of minds, poetry's townland.

VIII

Though College Square in Belfast and the Linen Hall
Had been our patch, nobody mentioned William Drennan.
In Dublin what dreams of liberty, the Index, the Ban:
Etonians on Commons cut our accents with a knife.
When Brendan from Ballylongford defied the Bishop, we
Flapped our wings together and were melted in the sun.

IX

A bath-house lotus-eater – fags, sodden *Irish Times* –
I tagged along with the Fabians, to embarrass Church
And State our grand design. Would-be class-warriors
We raised, for a moment, the Red Flag at the Rubrics,
Then joined the Civil Service and talked of Civil Rights.
Was Trinity a Trojan Horse? Were we Greeks at all?

X

'The Golden Mean is a tension, Ladies, Gentlemen,
And not a dead level': the Homeric head of Stanford
Who would nearly sing the first lines of the *Odyssey*.
That year I should have failed, but, teaching the *Poetics*,
He asked us for definitions, and accepted mine:
'Sir, if prose is a river, then poetry's a fountain.'

XI

Someone has skipped the seminar. Imagine his face,
The children's faces, my wife's: she sat beside me then
And they were waiting to be born, ghosts from a future
Without Tom: he fell in love just once and died of it.
Oh, to have turned away from everything to one face,
Eros and Thanatos your gods, icicle and dew.

XII

Walking forwards into the past with more of an idea
I want to say to my friends of thirty years ago
And to daughters and a son that Belfast is our home,
Prose a river still – the Liffey, the Lagan – and poetry
A fountain that plays in an imaginary Front Square.
When snow falls it is feathers from the wings of Icarus.

SNOW BUNTING

for Sarah

At Allaran, the otters' rock, between the breakers'
Uninterrupted rummaging and – from the duach –
Larksong, I mistake your voice for your mother's voice
Deciphering otter prints long before you were born

As though you were conceived in a hayfield so small
Stone walls surrounded a single stook, and the snow
Bunting's putative tinkle from beyond the ridge
Sounded even closer than the spindrift's whispering.

THE OAR

I am meant to wander inland with a well-balanced oar
Until I meet people who know nothing about the sea
– Salty food, prows painted purple, oars that are ships'
Wings – and somebody mistakes the oar on my shoulder
For a winnowing fan:
                                        the signal to plant it in the ground
And start saying my prayers, to go on saying my prayers
Once I'm home, weary but well looked after in old age
By my family and friends and other happy islanders,
And death will come to me, a gentle sea-breeze, no more than
An exhalation, the waft from a winnowing fan or oar.

OUT THERE

Do they ever meet out there,
The dolphins I counted,
The otter I wait for?
I should have spent my life
Listening to the waves.

ACKNOWLEDGEMENTS

The poems in this selection are taken from the following publications: *No Continuing City* (Macmillan, Gill and Macmillan, and Dufour Editions, 1969); *An Exploded View* (Victor Gollancz, 1973); *Man Lying on a Wall* (Victor Gollancz, 1976); *The Echo Gate* (Secker & Warburg, 1979); *Selected Poems 1963–1980* (Wake Forest University Press, 1981); *Poems 1963–1983* (Salamander Press, Gallery Press, 1985, Penguin Books, 1986, Wake Forest University Press, 1987, Secker & Warburg, 1991); *Gorse Fires* (Secker & Warburg, Wake Forest University Press, 1991); *The Ghost Orchid* (Jonathan Cape, 1995, Wake Forest University Press, 1996).